A DEMOCRACY, IF
WE CAN TEACH IT

McCourtney Institute for Democracy

The Pennsylvania State University's McCourtney Institute for Democracy (http://democracyinstitute.la.psu.edu) was founded in 2012 as an interdisciplinary center for research, teaching, and outreach on democracy. The institute coordinates innovative programs and projects in collaboration with the Center for American Political Responsiveness and the Center for Democratic Deliberation.

Laurence and Lynne Brown Democracy Medal

The Laurence and Lynne Brown Democracy Medal recognizes outstanding individuals, groups, and organizations that produce exceptional innovations to further democracy in the United States or around the world. In even-numbered years, the medal spotlights practical innovations, such as new institutions, laws, technologies, or movements that advance the cause of democracy. Awards given in odd-numbered years highlight advances in democratic theory that enrich philosophical conceptions of democracy or empirical models of democratic behavior, institutions, or systems.

A DEMOCRACY, IF WE CAN TEACH IT

EDUCATING THE NEXT GENERATION OF CITIZENS

THE HONORABLE MARJORIE O. RENDELL

CORNELL UNIVERSITY PRESS

Ithaca and London

Open access edition funded by the McCourtney Institute for Democracy at
Pennsylvania State University

First published 2025 by Cornell University Press

Library of Congress Control Number: 2025945753

ISBN 9781501789090 (paperback)
ISBN 9781501789106 (pdf)
ISBN 9781501789113 (epub)

GPSR EU contact: Sam Thornton, Mare Nostrum Group B.V., Mauritskade
21D, 1091 GC, Amsterdam, NL, gpsr@mare-nostrum.co.uk.

Contents

A DEMOCRACY, IF
WE CAN TEACH IT

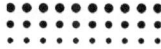

1

Civics Education: The Current State of Affairs

It may be an easy thing to make a Republic; but it is a very laborious thing to make Republicans; and woe to the republic that rests upon no better foundations than ignorance, selfishness, and passion.

—Horace Mann, 1848

More than 170 years ago, Horace Mann, often referred to as the father of American education, told us that the best way to preserve and sustain our democratic society and avoid the governance pitfalls of the Old World was to have an educated citizenry. We have failed to heed his advice. A recent report funded by the National Endowment for the Humanities, *Educating for American Democracy*, found that "the United States stands at a crossroads of peril and possibility. . . . We, as a nation, have failed to prepare young Americans for self-government, leaving the world's oldest constitutional democracy in grave danger, afflicted by both cynicism and nostalgia, as it approaches its 250th anniversary." Over the past two decades, our nation's civic knowledge and participation have steadily declined—leaving the world's oldest constitutional democracy alarmingly unprepared for the challenges of self-government. The Rendell Center was formed to help address these concerns and ensure that the next generation has the knowledge, skills, and dispositions of effective citizens.

The failures in civics education that we are working to address are newly urgent. Despite unprecedented access to information, young Americans are increasingly disillusioned, disconnected, and doubtful that civic participation has any real impact. A 2024 national survey conducted by the Partnership for Public Service indicated that overall trust in the federal government is at an all-time low, with the decline most severe among young adults aged 18–34; in this population, trust dropped from 30 percent in 2022 to 15 percent in 2024. Membership in civic groups and volunteerism have plummeted too, especially among young people and those without college degrees. These are not just abstract figures—they are warning signs of a democracy sick at its roots. In an age of polarization, misinformation, and declining institutional trust, civics education is no longer optional. It is urgent. If we do not teach the next generation what democracy is and how to preserve it, we risk losing it altogether.

I used to see it in classrooms all the time—students' eyes would glaze over when they heard I was there to talk about the Constitution. As a district court judge, I saw it in the eyes of jury members as they walked into the courthouse, confused and unfamiliar with the proceedings; by the end of their jury service, most would remark to me how transformed they felt by the experience, an incredible one that everyone should experience at least once in their lives.

For these reasons, I started working to promote civics education when my ex-husband, Ed Rendell, became governor of Pennsylvania. In 2000, when I was first lady of Pennsylvania as well as a federal judge, I heard Justice David Souter speak at a Court of Appeals conference. He related a story about a Russian lawyer who visited the Supreme Court and wanted a tour. Justice Souter volunteered to take him through the building and was surprised at the lawyer's knowledge of Supreme Court opinions. He inquired how the lawyer knew so much about the Supreme Court's work. The lawyer replied that during the Cold War when he or one of his lawyer friends got their hands on one of the opinions, they would meet clandestinely and discuss it. The lawyer then asked Justice Souter what he thought was the most impactful Supreme Court opinion of the modern era. Justice Souter immediately replied that it was *Brown v. Board of Education*. The lawyer looked disappointed. So, Justice Souter asked him the same question. The visitor responded, "The Nixon tapes decision, because in my country, the idea

3

that the head of government could be told what to do by the courts is unheard of." At that moment, Justice Souter had an epiphany: In America, we do not teach our children civics the way we should, nor how amazing our government is.

Like Justice Souter, two epiphanies sparked my interest in imparting civics knowledge to American citizens. The first was a naturalization ceremony. I performed the ceremony on July 3 on the lawn overlooking Independence Hall. Looking out at the new citizens—seventy-two of them from nineteen countries—I realized how much they appreciate America's democratic form of government. They have studied and learned about it. They left their countries of origin to come here because of the liberties and opportunities that our democracy affords them. Americans born on US soil are largely ignorant about how our government operates, let alone how special its workings are.

During my tenure as First Lady of Pennsylvania and even now, as I talk to students, particularly young students, they have passion and an inquisitive mind that we need to encourage. This became one of the driving forces behind the Rendell Center—to educate and inspire the next generation. My second epiphany, the other inspiration for promoting civics education, was a play, *The Trial of William Penn*. The plot is set in the late 1600s, with William Penn and his religious followers locked out of their place of worship during a time of tension between the Quakers and Oliver Cromwell. Penn begins preaching in the public square

4

and is arrested and tried for disturbing the peace. The jury is impaneled, hears the evidence, and retires to deliberate. They are brought back into the courtroom, and they tell the king's representative that they can only find Penn guilty of speaking in a public place, which is not a crime. They are dispatched to continue deliberating, and after refusing to give the desired verdict, are deprived of food. Nevertheless, they steadfastly refuse to reach the desired verdict. While often viewed as an example of jury nullification, for me, the story gave me chills. Twelve jurors can be a bulwark against tyranny. The jury model—to hear the evidence and reach a decision based upon that evidence—is a defining feature of our legal system; and knowing how many citizens resent the inconvenience of a jury summons and manufacture excuses to "get out of" their service, the performance made me want to do more to impart the value of juries and the system to which I have devoted my career.

Today, these experiences continue to inspire me to try to educate students about the workings of our unique system of government and prepare young Americans for their role as active, engaged citizens. (My not-so-secret hope is that they also will go home and teach their parents to look at jury service in a more positive way!) That is why, since 2014, the Rendell Center has dedicated itself to the mission of civics education—to ensure that the next generation knows how their government works and why it matters. We work to instill not only knowledge, but purpose, so that each student understands their role in this democracy—from jury service, to voting, to attending a town meeting.

Through Rendell Center programs like the Citizenship Challenge, students take on real-life constitutional dilemmas and practice deliberation, critical thinking, and respectful dialogue. Our Literature/History-Based Mock Trial initiative brings civics alive in elementary school classrooms by connecting classic children's books with courtroom simulations—helping young learners grasp the fundamentals of justice, fairness, and the rule of law. Our Read Aloud Program offers the opportunity for students to work on literacy while also meeting with and learning from on-the-ground professionals like lawyers, judges, police officers, firefighters, and veterans. These experiences have sparked meaningful engagement in thousands of students across Pennsylvania and beyond.

This is the story of the Rendell Center—its vision, its commitment, and its work over the past decade to help make not just a republic, but republicans in the truest sense: citizens worthy of the democracy they inherit. When Elizabeth Willing Powell asked Benjamin Franklin at the close of the Constitutional Convention, "Well, Doctor, what have we got, a republic or a monarchy?" he responded, "A republic, if we can keep it."[1] The way to keep it is through educating the next generation, and this is how we're doing it: by working with students to ensure they have what it takes to be excellent citizens and excellent leaders tomorrow.

2

Revitalizing American Democracy: Why Civics Education Matters Now More Than Ever

The need for robust, high-quality civics education in the United States has never been more urgent. Such education—teaching students how government works, what their rights and responsibilities are, and how they can engage in democratic processes—is not a luxury. It is a necessity for our republic's health. Over the past several decades, as standardized testing focused heavily on math and literacy and as funding and instructional time grew increasingly limited, civics instruction has been pushed to the margins. Today, only a handful of states require a full year of high school civics, and many students graduate with little understanding of how government works or why their voice matters. Just five cents is spent per student on civics education for every fifty dollars spent on STEM education. According to the National Assessment of Educational

Progress, only 22 percent of American students scored at or above the "proficient" level in civics in 2023.[2]

Public schooling in the eighteenth and nineteenth centuries was offered in part to ensure that citizens would be equipped to participate meaningfully in a democracy. The connection between education and democracy is deeply rooted in American history.[3] From the founding era, leaders such as Thomas Jefferson and John Adams emphasized the importance of an educated citizenry. Jefferson, in particular, underscored the need to "illuminate, as far as practicable, the minds of the people at large."[4] He argued that liberty could not survive without a population capable of understanding and participating in self-government. George Washington similarly "urged for the expansion of education as essential to the perpetuation of the new nation's common values and the chance of a 'permanent union.'"[5] The founders' belief in the importance of civics education grew out of even older ideas about democracy. In ancient Greece, the concept of *paideia* referred to a holistic education designed to shape responsible and knowledgeable citizens.[6] Education was considered essential not just for individual self-development but for the health of the community. Thus, for most of the twentieth century, American civics was considered a core subject alongside reading, writing, and arithmetic. Students learned about the Constitution, discussed current events, and even practiced civic participation through student government and mock trials.

Against the declines of the past two decades, three major reports have shaped the national conversation around how schools can renew their preparation of students for their vital role as citizens.[7] Each report, produced by leading civic and academic institutions, reflects its historical moment and responds to evolving challenges. But taken together, they offer a roadmap for renewing civics education and fortifying American democracy.

I will discuss the most recent pair in a future section, but the earliest of the three, *The Civic Mission of Schools* (2003), was seminal in helping us develop the eventual methodology of the Rendell Center. The report emerged in response to the narrowing of the school curriculum under the weight of standardized testing. Published by the Carnegie Corporation of New York and the Center for Information & Research on Civic Learning and Engagement (CIRCLE), the report warned that those in charge of adopting standards and developing curricula in the schools were pushing civics education to the margins, even though the very purpose of public education in our democracy is to cultivate engaged citizens.

The report laid out six "proven practices" of civics education, emphasizing both content knowledge and participatory learning: (1) formal instruction in government and history, (2) discussions of current events, (3) service learning, (4) extracurricular activities with civic purposes, (5) student involvement in school governance, and (6) simulations of democratic processes like mock trials and debates.[8] The report called on educators and policymakers to reassert civics learning as a central mission of schooling. It served as a clarion call to restore the subject to its rightful place in the K–12 curriculum. It emerged at a time when schools, under pressure from federal mandates like No Child Left Behind, had narrowed their focus to testable subjects: reading and math. This report laid the groundwork for PennCORD—the Pennsylvania Coalition for Representative Democracy, an initiative I started when I was First Lady of Pennsylvania. PennCORD was the precursor to the Rendell Center for Civics and Civic Engagement, and it taught us some valuable lessons about what works.

Pause to consider just how broad in scope our effort would need to be to touch an entire generation—it's hard to imagine! To spark a nationwide movement to restore the civic mission of schools, the National Conference of State Legislatures, the Center on Congress at Indiana University, and the Center for Civic Education joined forces as the Alliance for Representative Democracy. From 2003 to 2006, the coalition sponsored a series of national summits on the critical role civics education plays in fostering active, informed citizenship. These summits, known as the Congressional Conferences on Civics Education, were funded by the United States Department of Education, and the four leaders of the United States Congress served as cohosts. Delegations from all fifty states attended the Congressional

Conferences and were composed of elected officials, policymakers, and educators. The Congressional Conferences resulted in fifty state campaigns to restore the civic mission of schools and promote civics education. PennCORD was one of these state initiatives.

PennCORD

In Pennsylvania, we established the Pennsylvania Coalition for Representative Democracy (PennCORD) in response to these conferences and the work of the Corporation for the Civic Mission of Schools. It was a partnership between my office, the Office of the First Lady of Pennsylvania, the Pennsylvania Bar Association, and the National Constitution Center. Formally engaging institutional players in this way is crucial to ensuring the breadth, depth, and longevity of civics learning, given the manifold interests at play in public education, which often pull students and educators in various directions.

PennCORD's mission was to reinvigorate civic engagement and learning among Pennsylvania K–12 students. In addition to organizations across the fields of education, advocacy, and government, it featured a coalition of over 133 public and private schools. We defined active civics learning as the integration of three learning spheres: civics knowledge, public action, and democratic deliberation. To accomplish our work, PennCORD received a grant from the Annenberg Foundation, showing that any such effort also needs to be well-funded.

Through PennCORD, we were able to implement civics education programs at schools across the Commonwealth. We were able to host workshops for students and teachers in partnership schools. These workshops stressed the six promising practices from *The Civic Mission of Schools* report and focused on how to achieve outstanding results. By the time our work ended, PennCORD was only able to touch a small sample of the schools that make up Pennsylvania's 581 school districts. And most of our efforts were to persuade the powers that be—from superintendents to principals and teachers—that teaching civic values was essential, rather than actually interacting with students or adopting specific programs.

However, the effort laid the foundation for the Rendell Center and our work. For we learned exactly what we were up against. Effectuating change in education is challenging. There would be a million excuses for not putting civics learning back into the already overcrowded school day. We knew we had to come up with ways to impart civics knowledge in spite of constraints. As you will see, our efforts would ultimately connect the Rendell Center with outstanding educators across the Commonwealth and partner organizations that we are still working with today, such as the National Constitution Center, the Heinz History Center, the Supreme

Court of Pennsylvania, and the Pennsylvania Council for the Social Studies.

Reports on Progress

We've discussed how the publication of *The Civic Mission of Schools* led to a national summit and sought to address the problems brought on by standardized testing. Eight years after that report's publication, the *Guardian of Democracy* report (2011) reaffirmed the six proven practices and presented them as more urgent than ever. Also spearheaded by Carnegie, CIRCLE, and the Campaign for the Civic Mission of Schools, this report framed civics education as a national imperative not only for democratic participation but also for economic competitiveness, social cohesion, and national security.[9] It placed stronger emphasis on equity, noting the widening civics knowledge gap among youth, particularly students of color and those from low-income backgrounds. It also updated the definition of civics competence to include twenty-first-century skills such as media literacy, digital engagement, cross-cultural communication, and civil dialogue.[10] The report pushed for systemic reforms, including incorporating civics into state accountability systems, expanding teacher preparation, investing in research, and promoting public–private partnerships to support civics learning.

A decade later, *Educating for American Democracy* (2021) responded to a political climate marked by increasing polarization, disinformation, and a fragile public trust in institutions. Funded by the National Endowment for the Humanities and the U.S. Department of Education, this effort brought together over 300 scholars and educators to develop a K–12 roadmap that integrates history and civics education. Rather than offering specific curriculum content, the report proposed a vertically integrated framework built around inquiry, reflection, and complexity. It emphasized teaching students to grapple with difficult questions and understand diverse perspectives.[11] Central to this roadmap were themes such as constitutional democracy, civic pluralism, institutional and social transformation, and the ongoing challenge of building a "more perfect union." It called for a renewed commitment to civics learning that is interdisciplinary, culturally responsive, and accessible to all students beginning in the early grades.[12]

While each report was shaped by its era, their common thread is unmistakable: All argue that schools play a critical role in sustaining democracy and that the programs formed in the crucible of the 2003–2006 summits had not yet touched enough classrooms. The 2003 report initiated the conversation by identifying proven classroom practices. The 2011 update deepened the analysis by placing civics learning within broader national concerns and stressing the need for systemic support. The 2021 roadmap moved beyond lists of practices and embraced a holistic, inquiry-based approach rooted in historical understanding and civic identity formation.

Together, these reports reflect an evolving understanding of what civics education must be, against continued and evolving challenges in America. Civics is not merely about memorizing facts or performing community service; it is about preparing students to think critically, participate constructively, and care deeply about the democratic experiment. At a time when civic trust is eroding and misinformation and polarization are rampant, these reports offer not only a warning but a vision: a society where every student is equipped to be a guardian of democracy.

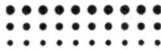

3

The Rendell Center for Civics and Civic Engagement

Afer the Rendell administration came to a close, Ed Rendell and I decided to continue the PennCORD work with our own nonprofit organization. In 2014, we incorporated the Rendell Center with a mission to promote civics education and civic engagement. The Rendell Center offers opportunities for the broader community to develop the knowledge, practices, and dispositions of engaged citizenship. For educators, the Rendell Center creates curriculum content, pedagogical tools, and professional development experiences. And for students, the Rendell Center develops literacy-based programs and experiential learning exercises. From the start, we did not want to be constrained by geography, so we decided to make everything available online and freely downloadable from anywhere.

As we started the Rendell Center, we had a terrific team around us. Our founding executive director was my chief of staff for the last three years of the Rendell Administration, and she had also led my civics initiative and PennCORD. Our board of directors, although small, included several top educators and policy people as well as longtime colleagues, each of whom brought a unique perspective to the board but was equally passionate about civics education.[13]

Our lessons learned in PennCORD helped shape our vision for the Rendell Center. We had listened to teachers during PennCORD, and we would also apply what I had learned during classroom visits as first lady, such as the fact that we need to produce programs and lesson plans that fit within the curriculum and not be an add-on or burden. Teachers already have enough on their plates. They also need content knowledge more than pedagogy; most know how to develop lesson plans, but they do not have a background in the content. They need help in bringing the content to life once they have the background knowledge. Programs need to be engaging—full of experiential learning instead of rote memorization. They need to challenge the students and relate to the world. We have learned that students spend much of their days passively listening to lectures or videos. So, simply adding more reading material or lectures is ineffective (we've seen students nod off when some of our volunteer lawyers focus too much on lecture and not enough on hands-on learning). When students get up and deliver opening statements in a mock trial or ask questions as though they are Supreme Court justices at oral argument, they are forced to move, which gets their blood pumping and their brains working!

Additionally, our focus has been on young students. High school students were not as interested in discussions of the Constitution, as if they'd already inferred from a lifetime without civics education that the topic must be boring and ignorable. One exercise still haunts me. In a high school class in Harrisburg, Pennsylvania, I asked the students to come up with something in their lives that is not affected by the Constitution. Dead silence. Not a single hand went up. So, I reached for a tried-and-true change of subject: an invitation to "stump me" as a federal judge. Still nothing. They were fully tuned out, and nothing I did could spark their interest. However, it was a learning experience for *me*. When we took those same exercises into a fourth-grade classroom, young students' hands went up time and again, eager to answer questions and engage with us, even after the class ended. Civics is not boring—but young adults have come of age in a system that has led them to believe otherwise.

To make a difference, we chose to focus on elementary schools because we wanted to take advantage of the excitement that younger children bring to the learning environment. At the stage when children are learning the importance of individual responsibility, cooperation, respect for others, and the importance of being part of a team, they can also be encouraged to self-identify as citizens. It is the perfect time to lay the foundation for engaged citizenship later.

Quite often, we underestimate children's ability to take in the concepts. When I was first lady of Pennsylvania, I visited Allentown's Ritter Elementary School as part of our "First Lady Civics First" bus tour. Allentown is not a wealthy community. Quite the contrary, in 2023, more than one in five families were living in poverty. We were invited by the Center for Civic Education, which developed the School Violence Prevention Demonstration (SVPD) program. Its goal was to explore ways in which civics education could be used as a strategy to foster civic engagement, law-abiding behavior, peaceful conflict management, and the prevention of violence in schools; important and valuable lessons that are best to learn at an early age. The students composed and performed a rap song about authority, responsibility, justice, and privacy. Those terms—*authority*, *responsibility*, *justice*, and *privacy*—were part of the SVPD program, and the students had absorbed them easily, learning that they needed to master knowledge, skills, and develop certain kinds of attitudes to address public problems and be active citizens. They also learned that public institutions are likely to work better when citizens participate. The program was exceptional and met the students where they were with basic concepts upon which they could joyfully build.

After implementing the program, it was amazing to see how these fourth-graders understood the concepts and were excited about making them their own. A climate study conducted by the Center for Civic Education showed a positive correlation between higher levels of classroom implementation of the SVPD program and higher achievement levels on Pennsylvania standardized tests. When interviewed for the study, students said the most important concepts they learned were as follows:

- You have to share and respect.
- "No bullying" is important.
- Justice is important because it is about fairness and kindness.
- Privacy means that you do not invade others' privacy.
- Responsibility means you get your priorities straight.
- Responsibility means that there are consequences and benefits to being responsible.

The principal shared that one student, when sent to the principal's office for acting out in class, offered no excuses but readily accepted reprimand, stating she wanted to take responsibility for her actions. It was exceptional to see those elementary school students demonstrate their understanding of concepts that many adults do not grasp.

As we started the Rendell Center, we were excited to take these lessons and proofs of concept and apply them to our work and to our developing curriculum. But we soon learned a disappointing fact, which remains a challenge today: While we thought that our civics curriculum was research-based, engaging, and easy to incorporate, teachers weren't interested. They did not have the bandwidth to include our curriculum. They already had their days, weeks, and months planned; they had standardized tests to prepare for, and there simply was, as numerous teachers, principals, and superintendents put it, "no time." The thought of "making time" for civics got no traction, as civics and social studies were increasingly devalued as subjects that needed to be taught, for, as we know all too well, they are not part of the high-stakes testing regime in reading and math. So, adding more to an already overloaded curriculum was an uphill battle not worth fighting. Not many schools were as enlightened as our friends in Allentown.

Accordingly, we set our sights on activities that we thought teachers would be interested in, which involved trial and error. We developed activities that tied into subjects that were tested and not pushed aside. Thankfully, schools have been much more open to implementing these programs. Now, our three main student programs are these: Read Aloud Lessons, Literature/History-Based Mock Trials, and the Citizenship Challenge. All programs have a common tie to literacy, which is a testable and high-priority subject. We went through the stories taught as literature and found that many also hinge on a conflict through which we could teach a civics lesson. We saw this in Allentown with the SVPD program. I also saw this in fairy-tale mock trials that were being done across the Commonwealth by elementary schools (the trial of Goldilocks for trespassing is a classic law-related education lesson that has been replicated many times). Students read the fairy tale and then are able to act it out in a trial. Knowing its success, we made it a basis for our own mock trial program.

With our programs set, we assembled a talented group of five teachers whom we had known from our PennCORD days and began writing lessons and activities around the concept of using literature to teach civics. They produced a series of lesson plans and activities called We the Civics Kids, which became the precursor to our current Read Aloud Program. We then moved on to develop mock trials. The Center's first curriculum director was highly involved in developing our mock trial handbook and associated lesson plans.

Now it was time to pilot the programs. Early on, we had developed a relationship with the Edwin M. Stanton Elementary School in Philadelphia, and in 2016, they agreed to be our pilot school. Housed in a historic Art Deco brick building, the school serves K–8 students and is led by an inspirational principal and extraordinary teachers, all of whom believe in the need to infuse civics into the school. The building itself is inspiring too: as you walk through the halls and up the steps, you climb a stairway inscribed with important dates in history. In the gym is a mural of Philadelphia and playing children, and it displays the message, "Education breeds confidence, confidence breeds hope, and hope breeds peace." All through the three-story building is an air of excitement. We were struck by how quickly we bonded with the teachers.

Getting to work, we collaborated on developing an EM Stanton Constitution detailing the rights and responsibilities of the students and staff in the school. We also conducted mock trial exercises. We worked particularly closely with the two fifth-grade teachers and our staff would go into the classrooms on a weekly basis, highlighting literature and lessons with civics themes. The Rendell Center EM Stanton Pilot School Banner still hangs in the main hallway among posters of famous American political figures. Together, we wrote an elementary school curriculum and tested our lessons. Theirs were the first classes to do trials.

Fast forward a little, and in 2017, we conducted a research study on the impact of those lessons. The report showed that the students' content knowledge improved by 33 percent. One second-grade teacher found the lessons to be "overwhelmingly awesome," imparting an understanding of what it meant to be an engaged citizen and, she hoped, what students would need to become leaders in their schools and community. Another teacher was equally laudatory, calling the materials "awesome lessons" that—we were relieved to hear—"support the curriculum objectives for the district."

We are proud of the work we have done with EM Stanton Elementary School. We are still working with them. As our executive director walks through the hallways, students say hello by name. Some of these kids have known our staff since kindergarten. Indeed, as our programs have solidified around core successes, we now start with simple lessons as early as the K–2 level around eight themes: community, rules, choices and voices, American identity, leadership, rights and responsibilities, conflict and compromise, and youth activism. The lessons can begin with a read aloud of a children's book with discussion questions, then classroom activities such as writing a letter to a member of town council or congress; drawing pictures to thank first responders or making thank-you cards; continuing the discussion of problems the students might want to solve in their community; or interviewing a family member who was a veteran and doing an oral history. Our success at EM Stanton has shown that it is the partnership between the educator and the Rendell Center that makes the program work. Together, we can infuse civics education into the classroom not as an isolated lesson but as an integral part of the curriculum. I cannot say it enough: We need to work with the teachers, not just add more to their overloaded plates. This philosophy has aided the expansion of our programs in schools across Pennsylvania.

Read Aloud Lessons

When my son was little, I would read to him from Dr. Seuss, the *Curious George* books, or *Treasure Island*. His eyes would light up as I turned the pages. I never would have dreamed that the simple act of reading a book to a young child could shape not only their reading skills, but how they understand basic concepts such as rule of law, justice, rights, and responsibilities—yet I've seen it in hundreds of classrooms through the Rendell Center's programs. After ten years in the community, the Center has reached thousands of students across Pennsylvania through what has become one of our three signature programs: the Read Aloud Program.

Unlike the subject of civics, literacy is foremost in the minds of elementary school teachers. So, not surprisingly, our literature-based Read Aloud Lessons are one of the most popular programs for K–5 classes. This past year alone, over 9,000 students participated, and it grows by thousands each year. For us, it is an amazing number, but only a tiny dot when you think about the 1.7 million public school students in Pennsylvania—or the 49 million public school students in the US, or the additional private and parochial students whom the Rendell Center also serves.

This interactive program approaches civics education in an easily relatable way to elementary-aged students across the state and country. The classes have evolved from their early pilot days in one Philadelphia school; now they are hosted via Zoom by Rendell Center teaching staff along with guest lawyers, veterans, or first responders, depending on the monthly theme. Monthly themes are chosen based on civic holidays such as Constitution Day, Law Day, Veterans

Day, First Responder's Week, Election Day, Black History Month, and Women's History Month, to name a few. Books are chosen based on their applicability to each theme and age-appropriateness.

The books for the Rendell Center's read alouds are carefully chosen by educational professionals for age appropriateness, high interest, and entertainment value. We know that if it's not fun and interesting, students will tune out. Discussion questions are written by Rendell Center staff and designed to review key lessons from each book and meet students at their level of understanding. Active participation in an engaging discussion follows each reading—students are excited to answer questions about the book as well as ask related questions they might have. They hear firsthand from the honored guest what it's like to be in a war zone, or what it takes to be a judge, or what happens in a day in the life of a plaintiff or defense attorney.

For example, we love Michelle Knudsen's *Carl the Complainer*, a story about a boy who often whines and complains—then he realizes that he is able to effect change when he uses his voice in a positive way. *Carl the Complainer* teaches students how to become a change agent in their classrooms, schools, homes, and communities instead of whining and complaining like Carl. Carl's awakening happens when he decides to do something about the early closing of a community park; he decides to write a petition to keep it open later, and the petition succeeds. With its whimsical illustrations, this book is highly entertaining, and students become engaged because they can easily identify with at least one of the characters. A fun and enthusiastic discussion always follows, no complainers allowed! The discussion questions end with a Take Action Project. Students are challenged to come up with a list of activities they can each take to address a problem in their school or neighborhood. They're invited to select one and list the actions they would take to make changes. One fourth-grade class, after reading the book, petitioned the principal to change the cafeteria menu. This is citizenship in action!

Another book, *Noodlephant* by Jacob Kramer, is perfect for use during Law Day to introduce concepts of fairness, equal protection under the law, and the power of protest. It's the story of an elephant who loves noodles more than anything. She lives in a world ruled by kangaroos who strictly enforce unfair laws—especially one that says elephants are not allowed to eat noodles. When Noodlephant stands up for her right to enjoy noodles, the kangaroos throw her in jail. But Noodlephant is smart, resilient, and full of ideas. She leads a rebellion with her fellow imprisoned animals, using creativity, solidarity, and a passion for justice to challenge the unjust rules and change the system.

Students examine how laws are created and challenged, and then they consider how imaginative resistance can bring about justice. The students become passionate about the characters. We have even developed a mock trial around the story. Like many of the books we recommend, this one works for students in the K–5 grade levels with the reflection questions scaled up or down depending on the audience.

But it's not just about the book. Providing a setting in which students feel safe to express themselves and pose questions to the special guest sometimes fosters the class's most teachable and memorable moments. During a Veterans Day Read Aloud to a second-grade classroom, the guest reader was a Vietnam War veteran who unexpectedly welled up with emotion when asked by a student, "When you were at war, were you ever afraid?" He took a moment to compose himself and thanked the child for asking this question. He shared that in all the years since the war ended, no one had ever asked him that. Then he answered by saying that yes, there were many times he was afraid, really afraid. He told the class what he did to get through his fear and encouraged these children to do the same. By the end of his answer, the adults in the room were moved, some of them reaching for a tissue themselves.

One of our favorite read alouds involves firefighters and the reading of the book *Sprinkles* by Frank Viscuso. It celebrates volunteer firefighters as good citizens. Every young student loves having a firefighter come to their school and teach fire safety. But this particular read aloud adds an additional dimension to an exciting school visit: a discussion of citizenship. Students learn (from an actual firefighter) that volunteer firefighters respond at a moment's notice to help anyone, and that the first volunteer fire department is older than our country, formed in Philadelphia by Benjamin Franklin in 1736. (Benjamin Franklin described volunteer firefighters as "Brave Men, Men of Spirit and Humanity, good Citizens, or Neighbors, capable and worthy of Civil Society and the Enjoyment of a happy Government.") There are now more than 29,000 fire departments in the United States, with more than 1.1 million firefighters. And nearly 70 percent of these firefighters are volunteers. As many classrooms of students discuss in our read-aloud programs, these brave volunteers offer a great example of citizenship in action.

To ensure quality and consistency, the Rendell Center collects feedback from teachers and readers after each event. We are always most pleased to hear that what we offer fills a niche that is otherwise difficult to address. For instance, one fourth-grade teacher said after we visited his students, "While I think there are many resources out there to coordinate some STEM-based learning opportunities, there are far fewer focused on the social studies, civics, and government side of student learning." We also take care to provide guests who understand the range of needs in a classroom; one first-grade teacher expressed her appreciation that "when asking and answering questions, the readers and facilitators have been very patient with my students with special needs."

For a further sense of how we evaluate the success of these read-aloud visits, a 2024 Constitution Day Read Aloud was evaluated as follows by the participating schools:

- Communication prior to event: 100 percent rated it excellent
- Ease of accessing/connecting to Zoom: 100 percent rated it excellent
- Facilitator's ability to relate to class: 83 percent rated it excellent, 17 percent very good
- Clarity and expression of the reader: 68 percent rated it excellent, 32 percent good
- Relevant and interesting discussion: 83 percent rated it excellent, 17 percent very good
- Sensitivity to your class's answers/needs: 83 percent rated it excellent, 17 percent very good
- Overall impression of the session: 83 percent rated it excellent, 17 percent very good
- How likely are you to schedule again: 100 percent rated it excellent

Data from each read aloud is used to refine book choices, improve discussion guides, and expand outreach. The program has steadily grown in participation across Pennsylvania and beyond, with plans to expand into more schools each academic year. In 2022, 1,700 students participated in our Read Aloud Program. In 2023, 2,800 students participated—and in 2025, we have grown to over 9,000 students participating! Fifty percent of the classrooms participate in more than one read aloud.

Case Study: Voting and Election Read Aloud Initiative at Keystone Academy Charter School

Overview. In the lead-up to the 2024 presidential election, the Rendell Center for Civics and Civic Engagement partnered with Keystone Academy Charter School in Philadelphia. The administration wanted a dynamic way to introduce the election and the importance of voting to their students, so we developed a targeted Read Aloud Program initiative designed to teach elementary students about the importance of voting, elections, and civic participation. This program was developed to support the school's own mock election, a student-led vote to determine the best Philadelphia mascot— a fun, engaging way to mirror real-world democratic processes while grounding the experience in meaningful civics learning.

Keystone Academy Charter School is a public K–8 charter school located in the Tacony neighborhood of Philadelphia, serving approximately 660 students. The school is known for its racial and ethnic diversity, with a student population that is approximately 36 percent Black, 33 percent Hispanic, 18 percent White, and 7 percent Asian. Keystone serves a predominantly low-income population, with about 88 percent of students qualifying for free or reduced-price lunch. It is a Title I school with a student body that includes around 8.5 percent English language learners and 23 percent receiving special education services. Academically, Keystone faces challenges in math and reading, with proficiency rates around 22 percent and 50 percent, respectively. While the school performs well in science, proficiency scores in reading and math are below state averages.

Program description. Over the course of the 2023–2024 school year, the Rendell Center conducted a series of virtual read alouds for Keystone's elementary students (K–4), each one tied to themes of voting, leadership, civic duty, and participation. Volunteer readers—lawyers, judges, and civic leaders—presented a carefully curated selection of children's books and led classroom discussions using Rendell Center–developed discussion guides around civics themes. These read alouds were not standalone lessons, but rather part of a coordinated civics unit that built background knowledge and enthusiasm leading into the mock election. The lessons helped students understand issues such as the following:

- Why we vote;
- Who makes decisions in a democracy;
- How campaigns and elections work; and
- What it means to be an informed voter.

Students then applied what they learned in a mock election to choose the best Philadelphia mascot, with candidates including Gritty (Flyers), the Phillie Phanatic (Phillies), Franklin (76ers), and Swoop (Eagles). The school created campaign posters, held classroom debates, and conducted an official ballot vote—mirroring the democratic process in an age-appropriate, student-driven way.

Books featured in the read-aloud series included *I Voted: Making a Choice Makes a Difference*, by Mark Shulman; *Vote!*, by Eileen Christelow; *Grace for President*, by Kelly DiPucchio; *Duck for President*, by Doreen Cronin; and *If I Ran for President*, by Catherine Stier.

Each book provided a foundation for exploring voting rights, leadership qualities, campaign messages, and voter engagement. After each reading, students participated in lively discussions about campaign promises, voter fairness, and what makes someone a good leader.

The goals of the initiative were fourfold:

1. Build foundational knowledge: Help elementary students understand the voting process in a fun and accessible way.
2. Promote civic engagement: Encourage students to see voting as a responsibility and a right.
3. Support experiential learning: Connect classroom instruction to real-world democratic practices through a school-wide mock election.

4. Foster informed decision-making: Teach students to evaluate choices and make thoughtful, reasoned decisions.

Impact. The read-aloud series at Keystone Academy proved to be a powerful example of how civics education can be embedded into school culture—even at the elementary level. Students didn't just learn about voting; they participated in a democratic process themselves. The students were engaged from the early fall readings through the election, which featured a town hall with local college students describing the Presidential Mascots' themes. The parent association was also involved and helped set up voting booths for the students. Everyone voted. The students were excited and engaged. We were able to simulate the voting experience electronically and tally the votes. And in case you're invested in the outcome, Swoop won—because of his platform of better food in the cafeteria! It really showed the students were listening to the candidates. It was not just a popularity contest.

Afterward, one teacher praised the experience, mentioning, "They loved voting for the different options in the book. This lesson aligns with our current social studies curriculum." Another said, "Our students loved having to vote on a class pet and explain why." And what we really love to hear is how students engaged with the program! One third-grader said, "I voted for Gritty because he's funny—but I also listened to what my classmates said about the other mascots. It was hard to choose!" And from a fifth-grader: "We learned that some people didn't always have the right to vote. That made me think that it's really important when you do get to vote."

Conclusion. The Rendell Center's Voting and Election Read Aloud Series at Keystone Academy Charter School demonstrates how early civics education, when paired with engaging literature and student-centered experiences, can instill a lifelong appreciation for democratic participation. By combining storytelling, discussion, and action, the initiative turned young students into thoughtful voters, and laid the foundation for active citizenship for years to come. The teachers continue to be strong participants in our traditional read aloud series, and during the 2024–2025 school year, the Rendell Center continued to work with the school on a student council election.

Similar to the effect we saw in our Keystone Academy Charter School, studies show that the very act of reading aloud is one of the most important activities teachers and parents can do with children to build important foundational skills, model fluent, expressive reading, and promote feelings of belonging to a community. Research from the Warner School of Education at the University of Rochester found that spending just fifteen minutes a day reading aloud can build knowledge, strengthen connections, and set children on a path to long-term academic success.

Reading aloud to our English language learners holds even more benefits by promoting vocabulary and comprehension and advancing a sense of wellbeing, belonging, and empathy. Far from being a passive experience, regular read-aloud sessions engage students actively, stimulating imagination, enhancing vocabulary, and strengthening listening comprehension. Decades of research affirm that consistent read-aloud experiences contribute significantly to students' academic and behavioral development, particularly in the early grades. According to the National Early Literacy Panel (2008), early exposure to books and storytelling is strongly correlated with better language outcomes, including listening comprehension, which is a predictor of reading comprehension later in life.

As we saw in the testimonials from the Keystone Academy students, one of the most immediate benefits of reading aloud is the improvement of active listening skills. The act of listening to complex sentence structures, varied vocabulary, and rich narratives helps students develop sustained attention and auditory processing abilities. Additionally, reading aloud has a measurable impact on working memory—the ability to hold and manipulate information over short periods. When students follow a storyline, remember character names, and make predictions about plot developments, they are exercising their working memory. A 2021 study published in *Frontiers in Psychology* found that students who engaged in daily read-aloud sessions demonstrated statistically significant improvements in working memory tasks over an eight-week period compared to control groups who engaged only in silent reading.

The benefits extend beyond cognition. Reading aloud promotes shared community and classroom connection, encouraging discussion, empathy, and critical thinking. It introduces students to a broader world, offering diverse perspectives and experiences. The *American Academy of Pediatrics* has emphasized that reading aloud stimulates brain development, particularly in the areas responsible for language acquisition and executive function skills.

When professionals—lawyers, judges, firefighters, and veterans—read aloud to students, the benefits are twofold: young learners gain a deeper understanding of the world of work, public service, and civic responsibility, while the professionals themselves grow as civic leaders and community role models. Many elementary schools have a career development requirement, and exposure to our guest readers helps fill that requirement. When these experiences are led by professionals, students are also exposed to the real-world applications of learning and public service. The presence of a firefighter reading about teamwork, a judge discussing rules and laws, or a veteran sharing a story of service connects curriculum to life in tangible, meaningful ways. According to a 2020 report by the Learning Policy Institute, students who engage with community role models demonstrate higher levels of motivation and a greater sense of future purpose.

In addition, for students in underserved communities, these virtual visits may be their first direct interaction in a positive light with a lawyer or judge. When the lawyer or judge returns monthly, the encounters can help the students understand the judicial system and the courtroom. It can also help the student see themselves in that role. For instance, we have a United States attorney who regularly works with the Read Aloud Program and shares her experience growing up in a lower-income Philadelphia neighborhood with the students. The smiles and head nods that we see from the students show their engagement with the program and excitement that someone from their world has achieved success and is now taking the time to read to them on a regular basis. On the other side of the spectrum, we work with the American Board of Trial Advocates (ABOTA); as a national organization, the participating lawyers can come from anywhere in the country. Traditionally, students from Philadelphia have little exposure outside of their neighborhoods, so it is a profound experience for students from urban Philadelphia to interact with a lawyer from rural Texas or Louisiana, discussing commonalities or engaging in a friendly banter about football teams.

For the professionals themselves, reading aloud in classrooms supports both personal growth and career development. Explaining complex ideas in simple, engaging language sharpens communication and public speaking skills. Sharing personal experiences builds empathy and reinforces the values of service and mentorship. Participating in education initiatives also demonstrates a commitment to community investment—an increasingly valued trait in professions that rely on public trust and civic engagement. Moreover, programs that bring professionals into classrooms help them reconnect with the fundamental purpose of their work: to serve and protect the public, uphold justice, or defend democracy. In this way, reading to students is not just an act of service, but a reaffirmation of professional identity.

These read alouds help inspire the next generation of leaders and transform the classroom into a space of mutual respect, civics learning, and inspiration. In a society striving to build stronger civic bonds and more engaged citizens, programs that bring professionals into schools to read aloud are more than a nicety—they are a necessity. We are actively expanding our program to other states and looking for volunteers to read and connect with the students; we have also doubled the number of books identified as good texts, and we have designed additional discussion questions. These books and questions are free and downloadable on our website.

Literature/History-Based Mock Trial Program

Our Literature/History-Based Mock Trial Program is the crown jewel of our literacy-based civics education programs for K–8 students. The program is designed to focus on the literature and history that students are already reading and studying in the classroom, and it is easy to follow. The goal is to enrich the students' learning experience while teaching them about American government and the judicial system. The framework is one that marries literature, history, and civics literacy in an ongoing effort to provide students with the knowledge and disposition of engaged citizens. These are skills they will carry throughout their lives.

As we at the Rendell Center both believe and practice, the best way to experience a concept is to see it in action. So, let's see our Mock Trial Program in action at Philadelphia's Masterman Elementary School.

Case Study: Masterman Elementary Fifth Graders Put Dr. Benjamin Rush on Trial after the 1793 Yellow Fever Epidemic

Overview. At Masterman Elementary School in Philadelphia, two classes of fifth-grade students embarked on a transformative journey into American history and civics learning through a Rendell Center for Civics and Civic Engagement Mock Trial Program. Their case? The controversial role of Dr. Benjamin Rush during the 1793 yellow fever epidemic in Philadelphia, where they placed him on trial for involuntary manslaughter.

What made this experience unique was not just the historical subject matter or the dramatic setting. It was that the students themselves researched, wrote, and performed the trial. With guidance from Rendell Center educators and volunteer lawyers, these young scholars crafted an original script that explored science, ethics, public health, and justice.

Their culminating event took place in the prestigious setting of the federal courthouse in Philadelphia, where I was able to preside over the student-led trial. This hands-on experience bridged history, law, and civic responsibility in a way few classroom lessons can.

The historical foundation. The 1793 yellow fever epidemic was one of the most catastrophic public health crises in early American history. As fear and confusion gripped Philadelphia—the nation's capital at the time—Dr. Benjamin Rush emerged as one of the most active and vocal medical figures. His aggressive treatment methods, particularly bleeding and purging, sparked controversy. Some credited him with courage; others accused him of worsening the death toll.

This complexity made the case ideal for a mock trial. Students grappled with a powerful civic question: *Should a public leader be held accountable for the unintended consequences of their actions during a crisis?* The prosecution had to prove that Dr. Rush was aware of the unjustifiable risk associated with the events leading up to the death of many of his patients; that he did this by act or omission. Lastly, the prosecution would have to prove causation—that is, that a direct link exists between the negligent action and death of the individual. The trial was based on Laurie Halse Anderson's book *Fever 1793*.

The experience would prove memorable and valuable, as one fifth-grader, Mira, recapped: "During the mock trial . . . emotions ran high, friendships ran low, and we learned so much information about court. After the trial, I can tell you more facts than you would want to know about Yellow Fever, Benjamin Rush, and countless other things like court and being on defense. In the end, I took more than a handful (or 300 handfuls) of facts. I took experiences."

The process: research, writing, and role-play. Every mock trial begins with a teacher or administrator from an elementary school contacting the Rendell Center expressing interest in this experience for their students. This interest usually stems from a teacher development or information session conducted by Rendell Center staff throughout the year. During our first session with the class, the Rendell Center staffer, in partnership with an attorney volunteer, conducts a foundational lesson on rules and laws. The class begins with introductions and some background on the lawyer's education and practice.

The lesson then moves into a classic law-related education lesson, "No Vehicles in the Park." Students look at a rule that says no vehicles may enter the local park so that residents can enjoy the green space in peace. Even the youngest of students are able to articulate the need for such a rule and can relate it to what they enjoy doing in a park. Following that general discussion, various scenarios are presented and discussed. For example, "What about a trash truck needing to empty the trash cans in the park? Or an emergency vehicle trying to get to the hospital?" Students are asked what they think about the need to create exceptions and the rationale for doing so. Students play the roles of judge and lawyers in a mini court session on these scenarios. This initial exercise engages students and sets the stage for further lessons on courtrooms and resolving disputes.

Additionally, during this first lesson, terms and roles are defined. What does a judge do? What does a jury do? What is a defense or prosecuting attorney? What is the burden of proof? Who has the hardest role in the courtroom? In addition, time is typically allotted for students to ask questions about the law and the career opportunities. The next session is a short, scripted trial read by the students in a theater style to give them a feel for what happens in the courtroom.

In session four, the students begin diving into the topic of the trial. For our students in Masterman this year, it was Yellow Fever and Dr. Benjamin Rush. Students review and discuss the fact pattern: they are presented with charges for Dr. Rush, and we explore the law and the facts which support and oppose the conclusion that Dr. Rush is guilty. Typically, the children are divided into sides based on their initial views on the case. Often, we have the students line up along a Likert scale, where group 1 believes he is guilty and group 5 believes he is not guilty, and groups 2–4 are somewhere in the middle, and then the students at either extreme try to convince their in-between classmates to join their side.

With support from Rendell Center staff and volunteer attorneys, students began by diving into primary and secondary sources—letters by Dr. Rush, firsthand accounts of the epidemic, and research on eighteenth-century medicine and law. In collaborative teams, they explored legal principles, historical evidence, and persuasive argumentation. The students from this Masterman class even asked if they could take two weeks off from our sessions to do additional research. One student was so interested he asked his parents to take him to the Mütter Museum, a medical history museum in Philadelphia, to learn more.

In the next sessions, students are taught direct questioning techniques. They learn the difference between open-ended direct questions and leading questions; that is, between questions that do not suggest an answer, which invite the witnesses to tell the story, versus cross-examination questions that elicit only yes or no responses. The presentation of evidence through witnesses is reviewed, and the students themselves identify witnesses who will support or discredit the defendant. In small groups, with the assistance of attorney volunteers, students develop both direct and cross-examination questions. Each student brings his or her unique perspective to the case, enriching the experience with creativity and critical thinking.

Civics learning in action. This project offered rich, experiential learning. Foremost, students got firsthand exposure to legal concepts like due process and burden of proof, as well as courtroom procedures. The trial experience was steeped in history, too, deepening students' understanding of the early American republic, public health crises, and the role of leadership. They practiced valuable language skills such as writing, argument development, research, and public speaking. As a group activity, the trial required teamwork, leadership, and equity skills from start to finish, including collaboration, active listening, and respectful debate. And finally, it was an invaluable exercise in boosting self-confidence and engagement.

The volunteer attorney mentor said, "This experience lit a spark in many of the students—some of them are already saying they want to be lawyers or judges someday." And one student, Vincent, made this point even more eloquently:

I felt so glad that my classmates could express their emotions. On the other hand, many schools are neglecting history and civics classes, and millions of students around the world could be judges, lawyers, or just a passionate fan of civics. If schools could provide even more resources to curious kids, our world would be more civil.

Impact and legacy. The program reached its inflection at the federal courthouse in Philadelphia, where students presented their case in a real courtroom. It was an unforgettable opportunity for students to perform in an authentic legal setting, and their poise was outstanding. The 2025 Masterman prosecuting attorney, a fifth-grader, began:

And may it please the Court. Your Honor and Ladies and Gentlemen of the jury, I am and I stand with the Commonwealth of Pennsylvania. May I have your permission to move around the well? We are here today to prove beyond a reasonable doubt that Dr. Benjamin Rush is guilty of involuntary manslaughter with respect to the many who tragically died under his care. Sadly, he dishonored his vocation and violated the Hippocratic Oath during the epidemic by stubbornly refusing to acknowledge the deficiencies in his course of treatment.

This mock trial experience gave students more than just facts. It gave them a framework for acting confidently, thinking critically, and engaging thoughtfully in civic life.

One teacher whose class participated in Rendell Center's Mock Trial Program praised its superiority to a run-of-the-mill field trip to a museum or amusement park: "Students embarked on a true academic journey. . . . The assistant superintendent of the district said that this was the best learning experience he has ever seen in his thirty-one years in education."

The Rendell Center's History-Based Mock Trial Program gave these fifth-graders a transformative civics learning experience. By putting Dr. Benjamin Rush on trial, students didn't just explore the past. They practiced real-world decision making, persuasive communication, and responsible citizenship. As they step into the federal courthouse and into the shoes of legal professionals, these students are discovering the power of their voices—and their role in our democracy.

These are not isolated outcomes. They reflect the transformative potential of civics learning. It works in suburban schools and inner-city schools alike. In the fall of 2023, we began working with several seventh- and eighth-grade classes in a school in Chester, Pennsylvania, where teachers indicated that two-thirds of the students were reading below a second-grade level. When we first started the special mock trial initiative with the students, they could not name the three branches of government or answer simple questions about our government and history. We continued to work with the students, and by the spring of 2024, they had mastered an understanding of our Constitution and court system. They could define the roles in the courtroom (judge, defense attorney, jury, prosecuting attorney) and went from an unengaged group to active citizens.

Many teachers who have implemented the Rendell Center's Literature-Based Mock Trial Program have told us it presents a distinctive opportunity to engage their students in literature while at the same time improving their writing, speaking skills, and content knowledge about the judicial system and the Constitution. Moreover, they acknowledge that programs like ours help them establish a solid foundation of civics knowledge and understanding that will serve their students well into the future. Several have cited the improvement in pre- and post-test results for their own classes, some as much as 33 percent.

Mock trials are a prime example of experiential learning, which emphasizes active participation and real-world engagement. These structured, interactive experiences yield significant academic, cognitive, and civic benefits. Data from educational research consistently affirms that mock trials strengthen critical thinking, deepen content retention, and promote civic responsibility. When tied to literature or a historical event, it becomes even more powerful. Rather than passively absorbing information, students actively interpret primary sources, evaluate evidence, and apply legal concepts. According to the *National Council for the Social Studies* (NCSS), students retain more than 70 percent of the content learned through experiential simulations, compared to just 20 percent retained from traditional lectures. This hands-on lesson promotes deeper comprehension of complex ideas such as constitutional rights, the structure of the judicial system, and the importance of due process.

Mock trials help students develop essential cognitive and communication skills. Participants must think critically, formulate persuasive arguments, and respond in real time to challenges and counterarguments. A study by CIRCLE found that students who participated in structured civic simulations—including mock trials—demonstrated significantly higher levels of critical thinking and verbal communication than their peers. These skills are not only fundamental for academic success but also transferable to college, careers, and life as an engaged citizen.

Most relevantly, mock trials also promote civic knowledge and engagement. By stepping into the roles of lawyers, judges, witnesses, and jurors, students gain a firsthand understanding of how the legal system functions and why it matters. The Carnegie Corporation of New York's report, "Guardian of Democracy: The Civic Mission of Schools," underscores that experiential learning opportunities like mock trials are strongly linked to long-term civic outcomes. Students who participate in these programs are more likely to vote, follow current events, and see themselves as active participants in a democratic society.

Further, mock trials foster teamwork, leadership, and equity. These simulations require collaboration, as students must work together to build their cases, prepare witnesses, and strategize as a team. Students at any level can and have participated. It calls upon different strengths from public speaking, writing, research, or strategic thinking. This can boost self-confidence and engagement, particularly for students who may not excel in more traditional academic settings. Teachers report that the Rendell Center's Literature/ History-Based Mock Trial Program engages every single person in the classroom. It brings history to life, motivating students to return to their book to understand the motivation of a character as they write out the script.

I wish we could reach more students with this experience. The work our staff and attorney volunteers do in the classroom is labor- and time-intensive. We are hoping to expand our outreach with free downloadable scripted trials on our website and outreach to other bar associations and legal groups to help with the process. The reward for all this effort is in the students' excitement about civics, about how our judicial system works, and the role they played. They emerge with an understanding of what an important right a trial by jury is. And most of all, they understand that justice is the guardian of liberty.

Citizenship Challenge

The third program is the Citizenship Challenge, an essay contest for fourth- and fifth-grade classes. It began as a brainchild of Ed Rendell. He recalls how a fifth-grade boy shadowed him when he was mayor, asking many questions. He was curious about so many aspects of government, even the Constitution. Ed was taken aback at how thoughtful the boy's questions were and found himself so engaged by the boy's responses. He concluded that we underestimate the ability of younger students to think about what we consider to be complex subjects. Instead, he wanted to challenge and encourage those questions. This experience was the impetus for the Citizenship Challenge, and like us, we expect that you will be inspired and impressed by young people's understanding and comprehension.

Ed has always been able to synthesize his experience and turn it into programming to inspire students of all ages, and in this challenge, we pose a question related to civics and receive 500-word essays that take a position and support it. Past questions have included some tough ones:

- "Which part of the Bill of Rights do you think is most important and continues to exert the greatest influence?"
- "Should the Constitution be amended so that the President does not have to be a natural-born citizen?"
- "Should the Constitution be amended to eliminate the Electoral College system for selecting the President and be replaced with the national popular vote?"

In a 2023 article by *Scholastic*, students from Buckingham Elementary School discussed the contest. The question for eleven-year-old Cami Martin's class was, "What should be the 28th Amendment to the Constitution?" Her class advocated for term limits for members of Congress. Cami's classmate Colin Williamson said, "We need fresh ideas—some members have held their position for forty years." And Cami herself said, "I was really excited to get to work on such a big project and for our voices to be heard." The students pick the topic, do research, and the classes work as a team to produce the final essay. The essays seek to persuade—they advocate—something our children are not usually doing in school. And the students get to act as mini-adults, asked to opine on real issues.

The essays are then judged, and the top ten classes come to the National Constitution Center in Philadelphia to present a skit about their essay and answer questions about it. Those classes also tour the National Constitution Center, have lunch, and receive a civics library for their school. The first-place team wins $1,000 and the runners up receive $500; the Rendell Center covers costs of the trip to the National Constitution Center, admission fees, and lunch. The prize money is to be used for a civics project in their school. For instance, Buckingham Elementary used their money to take a field trip to Pennsylvania's capital in Harrisburg and meet with their elected officials. That is citizenship in action!

It is amazing how well-researched, considered, and persuasive the essays are. One year, we asked how we could increase the number of people who vote, and one class advocated putting ads on cereal boxes and painting over graffiti with pro-voting messages. The Challenge skits are remarkable too. One year, the question was: "The First Amendment in the Bill of Rights in the American Constitution guarantees individual rights and is a foundation for life in the United States. In your own words, explain the amendment, its importance to Americans, and indicate which freedom you think is most important and why?" One class acted out a boxing match between First Amendment Rights, in which free speech had the knockout punch against its counterparts. That year and others, many students have chosen to express themselves in song. One memorable skit advocating that we should retain the requirement that the president must be a natural-born citizen ended with the students singing Bruce Springsteen's "Born in the USA."

Case Study: Mr. Todd Serpico's Fifth Graders at Radnor Elementary Take the Citizenship Challenge

Overview. In this case study, we move our spotlight to the suburbs of Philadelphia, to the inspiring participation of Radnor Elementary School's fifth-grade class. It is led by teacher Mr. Todd Serpico, whose students have participated in the Challenge over the past ten years. In 2024, they advanced as one of the top ten finalists and demonstrated extraordinary teamwork, creativity, and civics knowledge.

As in years past, we opened the Challenge to fourth- and fifth-grade classes in public, private, parochial, and home study programs across Pennsylvania. We asked classes to write a collective class essay, which teachers submitted to the Rendell Center. The essays were evaluated, and the top ten to fifteen classes would then be invited to provide a final performance in support of their essays. While the competition alone generates much excitement among the students, the students are usually even more excited when they learn that their performances are broadcast on television (usually on the Pennsylvania Cable Network) and that a sports mascot (such as the Philadelphia Phanatic) will be in attendance.

That year, two hundred essays were submitted from schools across the Commonwealth of Pennsylvania. We invited the finalists to the National Constitution Center, where they performed songs, skits, and dances. At the conclusion of their performances, our special panel of judges (including Governor Rendell, a local celebrity or dignitary[14], and myself) questioned the students about their essays and performances.

Mr. Serpico's students' essay addressed the constitutional question that we posed to all the participants: "Should the Constitution be amended to eliminate the Electoral College system for selecting the president and replace it with the national popular vote?" The winning essay from Radnor looked at the historic background of the Electoral College and then succinctly discussed how the Electoral College was failing the Founding Fathers' vision of America in three ways:

First, in the end, the votes of only 538 delegates out of an estimated 337 million American citizens decide the next president, which leads to not all voices being heard and not all votes being valued equally. Second, voters living in safe and swing states have different interest levels in participating in the voting process. Third, the inequality of electoral votes and popular votes can result in the majority's candidate losing. Due to the inequality created in votes, we believe that the Electoral College should be abolished and replaced with the popular vote.

For the finals, the students collaborated to bring the essay to life in an original skit and musical performance that dramatized their points with special guest appearances from the founding fathers (in period costumes) and current presidents (in coat and tie). The performance was both humorous and thought-provoking, allowing students to show not just what they learned, but how they internalized core civic values. During the live Q&A, students from Mr. Serpico's class confidently fielded questions from judges.

The students won second place. The entire school celebrated their win in an assembly, and then the students were asked to present their skit to the Radnor school board, celebrating their achievement as well as the importance of civics and civic engagement.

Reflections and impact. For schools like Radnor Elementary, the Citizenship Challenge becomes more than a contest—it becomes a transformative educational experience that students remember for years to come. In a presentation at a Rendell Center event, a student five years after participating in the Citizenship Challenge talked about the experience of being a finalist and the effect it has had on his life. "The program helped expose me to a non-sports competition with a totally separate set of skills necessary," he said, going on to talk about the challenge of responding to on-the-spot questions from the judges. "It was because of this opportunity that I discovered my love for learning about the government of the United States, as well as governments of the world and world relations in general."

Participation in the Citizenship Challenge exemplifies what is possible when civics education is experiential, student-driven, and connected to real-world democratic practices. Through research, writing, performance, and civic dialogue, students not only learn about their rights and responsibilities—they practice them. The impact of the Citizenship Challenge can be seen in students' excitement as they present at the finals, but also in the hard work of developing the essays. Rather than just memorizing facts, the students have to work together on developing the essay and preparing for their presentation. The creative expression from the essay to the skit reinforces civic identity and confidence. And at the Challenge's final performance, where the spotlight is on public speaking and dialogue with professionals, the students are not intimidated when they answer the judges' questions; they are confident in their research and knowledge of the topic.

The Rendell Center's Citizenship Challenge remains a powerful platform for preparing the next generation of thoughtful, informed, and engaged citizens. Over the ten years of the Citizenship Challenge, we have reached over 30,000 classrooms. It could easily be duplicated across the country: While Philadelphia's access to the National Constitution Center is unique, there are manifold venues across the country that would be natural fits for such activities, and many are run by organizations that would be happy to host such a competition. Think of local historical societies, bar associations, local history museums, libraries, colleges, and universities. It could be integrated into county fairs, town hall meetings, rodeos, farm shows, and other community events. Such organizations and events are built by networks of community members and, thus, will have individuals who would be great fits for judges and staffers to promote and put on the challenge.

Measuring Results

So far, the Allentown Climate Study noted above was one of the only solid research initiatives to measure the impact of Rendell Center programs on student outcomes. We are currently working with the Annenberg Public Policy Center in Philadelphia (APPC) to help us assess the impact of our work more widely. With APPC's help, we are exploring how we can measure what our programs are doing, how we can expand, and whether we are effectively developing the skills necessary for the next generation. This has been a question surrounding civics education for years and a question I returned to repeatedly during my tenure as first lady.

How can we have an impact, short of creating a national initiative? It's something that APPC is working on by creating a Civics Renewal Network, the organization pursuing this mission and working along parallel tracks in an effort to accomplish change. We hope that Annenberg's research study of our programs will go beyond the letters and positive comments from teachers and students. I am excited about what it will uncover and how it will help us continue to improve and grow.[15]

For Ed and me, the Rendell Center has been a labor of love. It represents an opportunity to pass on our knowledge and our passion for what makes our democracy great by focusing young citizens on how it should work. An understanding of our democracy is crucial to our system's continued vitality. Educating students enough to understand their rights and responsibilities as citizens of the United States furthers this mission.

::::::::::

4

The Future of Civics Education: A Vision from the Center

I have been fortunate in my career to walk the same steps as the signers of the Declaration of Independence and the Constitution each day to the federal courthouse in Philadelphia. My chambers overlook Independence Hall and the National Constitution Center. I am reminded each day of the precious heritage we have and the remarkable documents that were forged more than 200 years ago. As I walk into the appellate courtroom in the James A. Byrne United States Courthouse, I look up and see etched in the ceiling, "Justice is the guardian of Liberty." Those six words are mighty, and I hope something of their power remains etched in the hearts of students who graduate from our programs.

At the Rendell Center for Civics and Civic Engagement, we believe the future of our democracy depends on what happens in our classrooms today. As we have discussed, civics education is not a luxury or an afterthought—it is a foundational component of public education and a prerequisite for a functioning, healthy democracy.

Since my early efforts in PennCORD and now with the Rendell Center, I have struggled with how organizations like ours can make a significant impact in the face of large-scale challenges such as political polarization, misinformation, and disengagement. Ed and I firmly believe the answer lies in our mission and methods, and in the power of education to shape the next generation of active, informed, and responsible citizens. As Ed said in his book, *A Nation of Wusses: How America's Leaders Lost the Guts to Make Us Great*, we need to demand more from our leaders and hold them accountable regarding the education of the next generation. "We've become a nation of wusses. We elect leaders who won't lead. We let politicians get away with dodging the hard decisions. And unless we change, we'll continue to fall behind the rest of the world." We need to be a strong force for civics education. Educators, nonprofits, members of the legal community, business leaders, parents, and students need to take a stand and remind our leaders who they work for. Our experience shows that this stand needs to happen at the local level to be effective. Ground up, not top down. From the People to the people in power.

While national conversations often focus on large-scale education reform or federal initiatives, it might well be that the future of civics education hinges on the sustained and strategic efforts of small nonprofits. As we approach the 250th anniversary of our nation, many local organizations are turning their focus toward civics. This turn presents a generational opportunity to harness these organizations' combined power, establishing and strengthening the connections among them. The Rendell Center is a leader in this work, and we want to help spread this approach.

In addition, our colleagues at the Annenberg Public Policy Center of the University of Pennsylvania have also been working since 2013 to strengthen the relationship among the many diverse civics education nonprofits through its Civic Renewal Network (CRN). The CRN is a nonpartisan alliance of around thirty-nine nonprofit organizations, and its mission is to enhance civic life in the US by improving the quality and accessibility of civics education, offering schools free, high-quality classroom materials. CRN collaborates with groups like the National Archives, Library of Congress, Khan Academy, and the Bill of Rights Institute to provide resources on voting, elections, media literacy, Constitution Day, and more. It also supports professional development, civic advocacy toolkits, and adult-education initiatives, such as grants to develop civics programs for military and community colleges.

Another important nerve center for coordination between nonprofits like the Rendell Center is CivXNow. Justice Sandra Day O'Connor formed an organization in

2018 that oversees this national coalition of organizations, mobilizing a push for strengthening and advancing civics education in the United States. Comprised of over 300 partner organizations—including educators, nonprofits, scholars, and business leaders—the coalition's mission is similar to the Rendell Center's, but it also advocates for policy changes at the federal, state, and local levels. It has been a hub for organizing between the forty states that formed state-level coalitions like PennCORD.

My hope lies with all of these small nonprofits whose work, like ours, demonstrates how local, mission-driven institutions can catalyze profound and lasting impact in classrooms and communities across the country. Our organizations have the advantage of flexibility, but when united by networks like CivXNow and the Civics Renewal Network, they may have an aggregate impact like that of a national program. Unlike larger bureaucratic institutions, small nonprofits are nimble. The Rendell Center can respond quickly to the evolving needs of educators, develop new content aligned with current events or curricular demands, and cultivate strong relationships with teachers, judges, lawyers, and community volunteers. This agility allows the organization to maintain relevance while fostering authentic civic engagement in real time. Furthermore, small nonprofits often serve as incubators of innovation. Our focus on mock trials and deliberative discussions, for example, fills a vital gap left by traditional civics instruction, which often prioritizes rote memorization over real-world application. These interactive experiences help students develop critical thinking, public speaking, and media literacy skills—tools essential not only for civic life, but for academic and professional success.

Besides participating in strategic partnerships like CivX-Now and the Civic Renewal Network, we can extend our combined reach even more by collaborating with bar associations, judicial systems, universities, and school districts beyond a single region. Moreover, digital platforms have opened up new opportunities for national outreach. Virtual read alouds, online teacher institutes, and downloadable curricula allow these organizations to scale their work while maintaining personal connections and high program quality.

Crucially, for small nonprofits to have a sustained and larger impact, they must be supported through consistent funding, visibility, and recognition. Philanthropic organizations and government leaders should prioritize investment in grassroots civics education efforts. Policymakers can also play a role by integrating these proven programs into broader state and federal education frameworks. At the same time, the future of civics education is not solely in the hands of large institutions or legislative mandates. Passionate teachers, community leaders, and parents must see themselves as part of the solution—as civic mentors who model curiosity, dialogue, and commitment to the common good. The future of our democracy depends on all of us.

As a small nonprofit, we understand the importance of being nimble, responsive, and deeply connected to the communities we serve. Our size allows us to work closely with those passionate individuals in community classrooms, tailoring programs to specific classroom needs and innovating quickly. We are not constrained by red tape—we are driven by mission. This flexibility has enabled us to continually pilot new programs, test creative approaches, and scale successful models through partnerships with school districts, bar associations, universities, and the judiciary. What we have tried to show in our case studies is a model of what is possible when a small organization is guided by a clear mission, a belief in democracy, and a commitment to empowering the next generation of citizens, and a willingness to collaborate. In doing so, it illuminates a path forward for civics education—one rooted in community, creativity, and courage.

We also know that impact is not solely measured in numbers, but in the depth of experience. When a fifth grader stands up in a courtroom to argue a constitutional principle, or when a second-grade class engages in a meaningful conversation about fairness after reading a civic-themed book, the seeds of democratic engagement are planted. These moments matter. And when replicated across schools, districts, and states, they build a culture of civics learning that can help restore the civic mission of American education.

At the Rendell Center, we are proud to play our part in this urgent and ongoing effort. The future of civics education is not a distant dream—it is a promise we renew every day in every classroom we serve. We hope you will join us and the growing network of people and organizations engaged in this crucial and exciting endeavor.

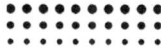

Acknowledgments

The Rendell Center's story would not be complete without sharing the influence and partnership of the Annenberg Public Policy Center (APPC). The APPC was started in 1993 by Walter and Leonore Annenberg. Its motto is "Research and Engagement That Matter," and its work has informed the policy debates around diverse topics—campaign finance, children's television, internet privacy, tobacco advertising, the tone of discourse in Washington, and disinformation. Scholars at the policy center have offered guidance to journalists covering difficult stories, including terrorist threats, suicide, mental health, the Zika virus, and vaccination hesitancy. APPC also manages FactCheck.org as well as Annenberg Classroom and the Civics Renewal Network, which it organized and manages. Annenberg Classroom has developed award-winning civics education materials for students and educators.

Ambassador Walter Annenberg and Lee Annenberg were our close friends during Ed's time in office. It was the Annenberg Foundation that helped with my PennCORD initiative. I think Lee would be pleased that we continued the fight for civics education and have a strong partnership with the APPC, led by Kathleen Hall Jamieson. We have also partnered on programs that explore judicial independence because a fair and impartial judiciary is a pillar of the American constitutional system. It guarantees that we are governed by the rule of law, rather than by the whims of the powerful. We are grateful for APPC's partnership and support over the years.

We extend our deepest appreciation to the volunteers who have given so generously of their time, talents, and commitment. Your contributions have enriched every aspect of our work and have brought meaningful civic learning experiences to students across the region.

We are especially grateful to the members of our board of directors, whose leadership and guidance sustain our mission and propel our growth. In particular, we thank our current board members: treasurer Sue Perrotty, members Jennifer Almquist Engelbrecht, Larry Brown, Donna Cooper, Tod J. MacKenzie, Jeffrey Marrazzo, Hon. Ted McKee, Alison Perelman, Jesse Rendell, Matthew Tom, and Gerald Zahorchak. We also thank our late member, John White.

To the educators who welcome our programs into their classrooms, we offer our heartfelt thanks. Your dedication to fostering civic knowledge and engagement among your students lies at the heart of what we do. Your partnership and innovation make our programs impactful and enduring.

We also extend sincere appreciation to my dear colleagues from the bench who have participated in our mock trials, moot court experiences, and classroom initiatives. Your willingness to engage directly with students, both in person and virtually, provides a rare and invaluable opportunity for young people to better understand our judicial system and the principles that underpin our democracy. Your collective commitment helps to realize the Rendell Center's vision: a nation of citizens who understand, value, and actively participate in our democratic system. We are honored to work alongside each of you in pursuit of this essential goal. Together we can make a difference.

Last, but not least, we thank our tireless executive director, Beth Specker, who has spearheaded this initiative since the days of PennCORD and whose efforts have transformed the passion and vision that Ed and I share into an actual, impactful, and multifaceted program. This program will educate and engage the next generation of citizens. To say we could not have done this without Beth is an immense understatement. Thank you, Beth.

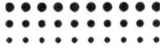

Notes

1   Julie Miller, "'A Republic If You Can Keep It': Elizabeth Willing Powel, Benjamin Franklin, and the James McHenry Journal," *Unfolding History: Manuscripts at the Library of Congress*, Library of Congress Blogs, January 6, 2022, https://blogs.loc.gov/manuscripts/2022/01/a-republic-if-you-can-keep-it-elizabeth-willing-powel-benjamin-franklin-and-the-james-mchenry-journal/.

2   "Eighth-Grade Scores Decline in Civics and U.S. History on the Nation's Report Card," *National Assessment Governing Board*, May 3, 2023, https://www.nagb.gov/news-and-events/news-releases/2023/eighth-grade-scores-decline-in-civics-and-us-history.html/.

3   Rebecca Winthrop, "The Need for Civic Education in 21st-Century Schools," *Brookings* (blog), June 4, 2020, https://www.brookings.edu/articles/the-need-for-civic-education-in-21st-century-schools/.

4   Maurizio Valsania, "America's Founders Believed Civic Education and Historical Knowledge Would Prevent Tyranny—and Foster Democracy," *The Conversation*, July 8, 2021.

5   David Davenport and Mark C. Schung, "Liberty and Civic Education," The Thomas B. Fordham Institute, November 16, 2023, https://fordhaminstitute.org/national/commentary/liberty-and-civic-education/.

6 Jack Crittenden and Peter Levine, "Civic Education," in *The Stanford Encyclopedia of Philosophy*, edited by Edward N. Zalta and Uri Nodelman (Metaphysics Research Lab, Stanford University, 2024), https://plato.stanford.edu/archives/sum2024/entries/civic-education/.

7 *The Civic Mission of Schools* (Carnegie Corporation of New York and CIRCLE, 2003), https://www.carnegie.org/publications/the-civic-mission-of-schools/; Jonathan Gould, Kathleen Hall Jamieson, Peter Levine, Ted McConnell, and David B. Smith, eds. *Guardian of Democracy: The Civic Mission of Schools* (Leonore Annenberg Institute for Civics of the Annenberg Public Policy Center at the University of Pennsylvania, 2011), https://www.carnegie.org/publications/guardian-of-democracy-the-civic-mission-of-schools/; Educating for American Democracy (EAD), *Educating for American Democracy: A Roadmap for Excellence in History and Civics Education for All Learners*, iCivics, March 2, 2021, https://www.educatingforamericandemocracy.org/the-roadmap/.

8 *The Civic Mission of Schools*, 20–22.

9 Gould et al., *Guardian of Democracy*, 10.

10 Gould et al., *Guardian of Democracy*, 14–18.

11 EAD, *Educating for American Democracy*, 1.

12 EAD, *Educating for American Democracy*, 20–27.

13 Particularly helpful are those board members who work with nonprofits that focus on youth, and those with entrepreneurial experience and creative backgrounds. We are constantly searching for new ideas as to how to spread the word, and the presence on the board of younger, tech-savvy directors has made a huge difference. Indeed, our board of directors has included a range of experts including, among others, plaintiffs and defense lawyers, general counsels, public school administrators, community bankers, public policy and planning executives, judges, nonprofit leaders, communications and marketing executives, community organizers, and college and university professors.

14 We have also had federal judges, a former US treasurer, the Phillies' COO, and CEOs of major companies serve as guest judges.

15 We are grateful to APPC and Kathleen Hall Jamieson for their support and guidance in this important task.

About the Author

Judge Marjorie Rendell is a senior United States circuit judge of the United States Court of Appeals for the Third Circuit where she has served since 1997. She was first appointed to the United States District Court in Philadelphia in 1994. She is also a former first lady of Pennsylvania. In that role, she became interested in civics education. She is now president of the Rendell Center for Civics and Civic Engagement and the winner of the 2025 Brown Democracy Medal.

www.ingramcontent.com/pod-product-compliance
Lightning Source LLC
Chambersburg PA
CBHW020345060326
40769CB00004B/880